CHINESE STORIES
FOUR MAJOR CONTRIBUTIONS

Chinese Porcelain

Edited by Li Chaodong

Illustrated by Xu Meng

Translated by Mingjiu Qi and Yan Wu

Books Beyond Boundaries
ROYAL COLLINS

We all know the word "China." When the letter "C" is capitalized, it refers to the country with a long history located in East Asia—China. However, when the "c" is lowercase, "china" refers to Chinese porcelain. Why does the same word have two completely different meanings?

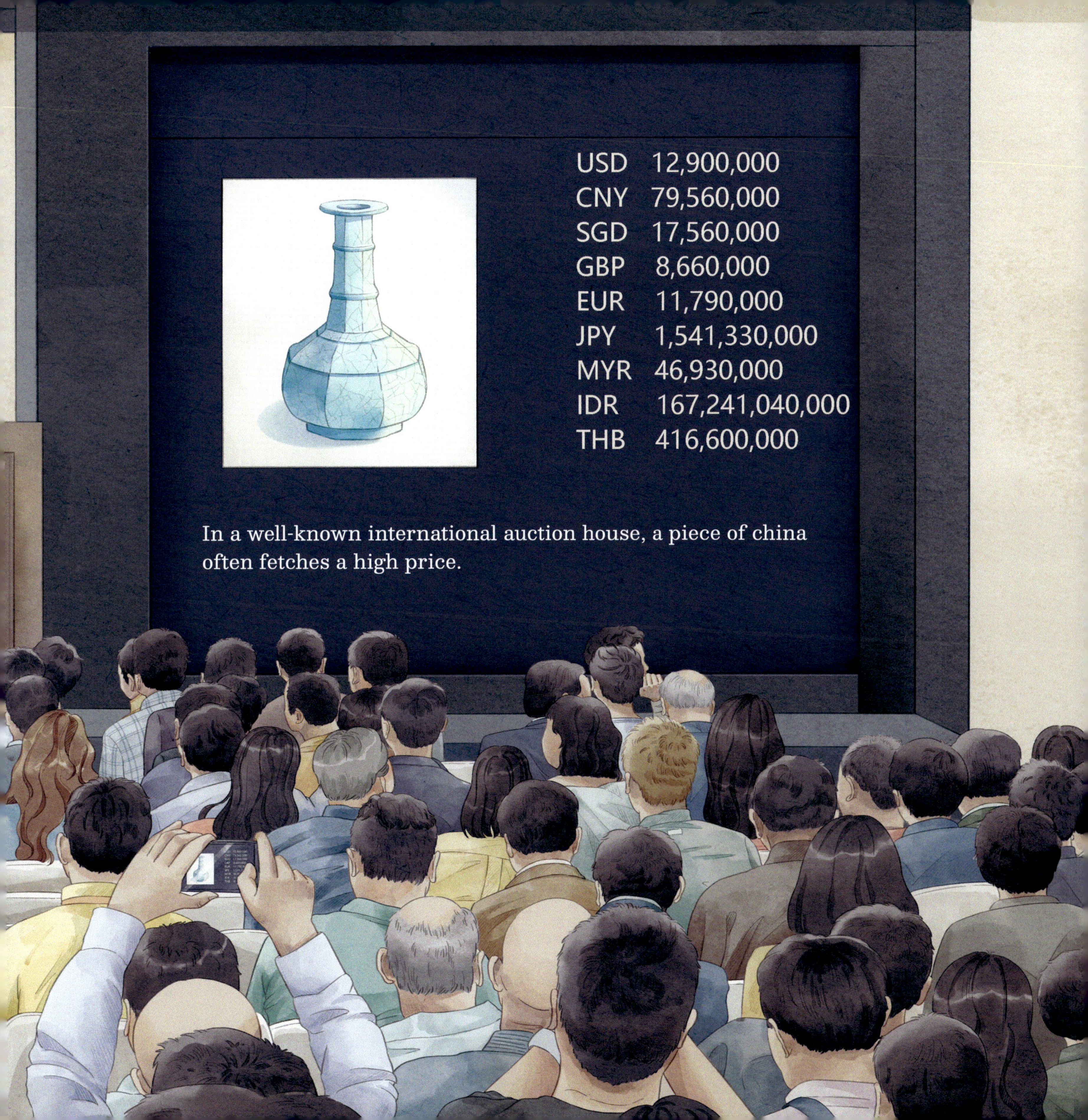

In a well-known international auction house, a piece of china often fetches a high price.

Chinese porcelain evolved from traditional pottery.

The ancient Chinese people spent considerable time working with clay in daily life. They discovered that mixing clay with water increased its stickiness, making it easier to shape. They used the mixture to fill in the gaps of baskets between the branches. But this method had drawbacks—once the clay dried, it became unstable and easily fell apart.

Eventually, our ancestors discovered that when these baskets were fired in a kiln, they didn't break down but instead became stronger. This marked the origin of pottery. At first, people crafted various containers for steaming food, storing grains, and holding water.

Brick

Wadang (a Chinese decorative tile)

Later, because pottery was strong and waterproof, people began making bricks and tiles for building houses. A remarkable example is "Qin bricks and Han tiles," referring to bricks and tiles produced during the Qin (221–206 BC) and Han (206 BC–AD 220) dynasties.

The increasing popularity of pottery also inspired creativity. People began shaping clay to imitate animals, humans, and various everyday objects, then firing them into beautiful works of art. Ancient people also painted patterns on pottery, giving us glimpses of their lifestyles and states of mind.

Terracotta Army of the Mausoleum of the First Qin Emperor

Figurines of the Han Dynasty

Court lady figurines of the Tang Dynasty

Octagonal star-patterned painted pottery of the Dawenkou Culture

Human-faced fish-patterned pottery basin of the Yangshao Culture

However, pottery's rough surface made it difficult to clean, and its tiny holes allowed liquids to seep through. To address this, ancient people began mixing plant ashes into clay and spreading the mixture on the surface of unfired pottery, creating the first plant-ash glazes. Later, lime glazes were invented, marking the birth of Chinese porcelain.

Purple clay teapot

❶ Picking clay

❷ Kneading clay

❸ Shaping clay

❼ Drawing patterns

❽ Glazing

❾ Loading in the kiln

Glazing techniques evolved after more than a thousand years of trial and error. By the time of the Eastern Han Dynasty (AD 25–220), porcelain-making skills had advanced.

Though the thin layer of porcelain may not seem like a high-tech invention, it was a cutting-edge technique unique to ancient China. It demonstrated the ancient Chinese understanding of heat levels and chemical reactions, comparable to modern chip technology.

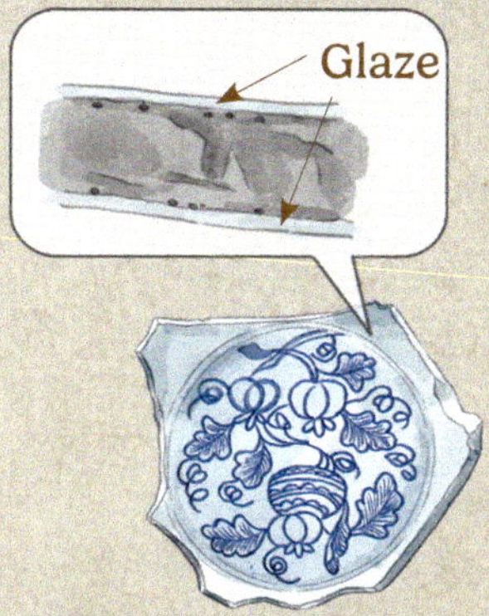

❹ Molding clay

❺ Trimming clay

❻ Drying clay

❿ Firing the kiln

⓫ Unloading the kiln

In the Jin Dynasty (AD 265–420), a porcelain spittoon (a container for spitting) became popular. General Wang Dun, frustrated and disheartened by the emperor's lack of trust, would often strike his porcelain spittoon with a jade stick, causing its edges to chip. Since then, the phrase "chipping the porcelain spittoon" has become a metaphor for frustration or disappointment.

During the Wei, Jin, and Northern and Southern Dynasties (AD 220–589), southern celadon and northern white porcelain were the most famous.

White porcelain from Xing Kiln

Celadon porcelain from Yue Kiln

Huzi (a container for holding water)

Unique items such as the chicken-head pot, porcelain spittoon, and *huzi* began to appear, and these even found their way into poetry and literature.

Sancai camel

In the Tang Dynasty (AD 618–907), finely crafted porcelain became a symbol of social status and began to reach Central Asia via the Silk Road. In exchange, Central Asian envoys brought fascinating items, such as camels and agate, to Chang'an, the capital of the Tang Dynasty. Central Asian culture and religion also entered China during this period, influencing porcelain art and creating the distinct "Tang *sancai*" (tricolored glaze).

Mise glaze plate

Among Tang Dynasty celadon porcelain, there was a type called "*mise* porcelain" (fine celadon porcelain), renowned for its jade-green color. It was considered the finest among Tang ceramics, inspiring even the great poet Lu Guimeng to declare, "It captures the green of a thousand mountain peaks."

The porcelain industry flourished during the prosperous Song Dynasty (AD 960–1279), with kilns producing porcelain throughout the country, each with its own unique characteristics.

Unlike the grandiose and monumental style of Tang porcelain, Song porcelain was more delicate and graceful.

Plain celadon narcissus basin

Ru Kiln produced porcelain with a light sky-blue glaze, simple and natural.

Square celadon vase

Official Kiln produced porcelain with a distinctive “purple mouth and iron foot,” evoking antiquity and elegance.

White glaze porcelain pillow

Ding Kiln was known for its white porcelain, which was dignified, elegant, warm, and serene, with various patterns and simple but intricate decorations.

Celadon pot with fish-ear handles

Ge Kiln produced porcelain with “ice crackles” on the surface, which were intentionally created by the craftsmen to give the porcelain a beauty of imperfection.

Rose-purple glaze begonia-shaped vase

Jun Kiln produced porcelain with colorful glazes, prized for their vibrant hues. It was said that “one color enters the kiln, and a thousand colors emerge.”

Besides the five famous kilns, numerous local kilns with distinctive characteristics contributed to the porcelain industry. The regions where these kilns were located soon became thriving commercial cities, attracting workers and merchants alike.

Due to porcelain's fragility, it was mostly transported by water. Jingdezhen, surrounded by water on three sides and known for its high-quality clay, has been called the "Porcelain Capital" since the Song Dynasty.

After the Song Dynasty, porcelain production soared, and prices decreased. Porcelain bowls, plates, cups, and spoons became common household items, remaining ubiquitous in present-day East Asia.

The vibrant, diverse porcelain culture and delicious cuisine contributed to creating a unique and rich Chinese food culture.

Throughout the history of porcelain, tea utensils played an important role. During the Song Dynasty, porcelain cups and tea bowls became popular tea utensils.

Rabbit-fur tea bowl from the Jian Kiln

From the black glaze tea bowls from the Jian Kiln of the Song Dynasty to the white glaze teacups of the Ming Dynasty (AD 1368–1644), porcelain tea utensils evolved to meet the changing tastes of tea drinkers. Along with the tea culture, Chinese porcelain spread overseas, gaining high praise from other countries.

White glaze three-tiered lidded bowl

Porcelain has evolved from a utilitarian object into a work of art that serves as a form of decoration. A single porcelain piece, or a carefully curated collection, can reflect the owner's lifestyle and cultural taste.

Due to its flat surface, ancient Chinese people often used porcelain as a canvas for poetry, calligraphy, and paintings. Folk tales were also depicted on porcelain in the form of comic strips, adding a layer of narrative and artistic expression to these everyday items.

The trade between China and overseas countries began very early. Initially, silk was the most sought-after commodity. However, after the Tang Dynasty, tea and porcelain became the main items in foreign trade.

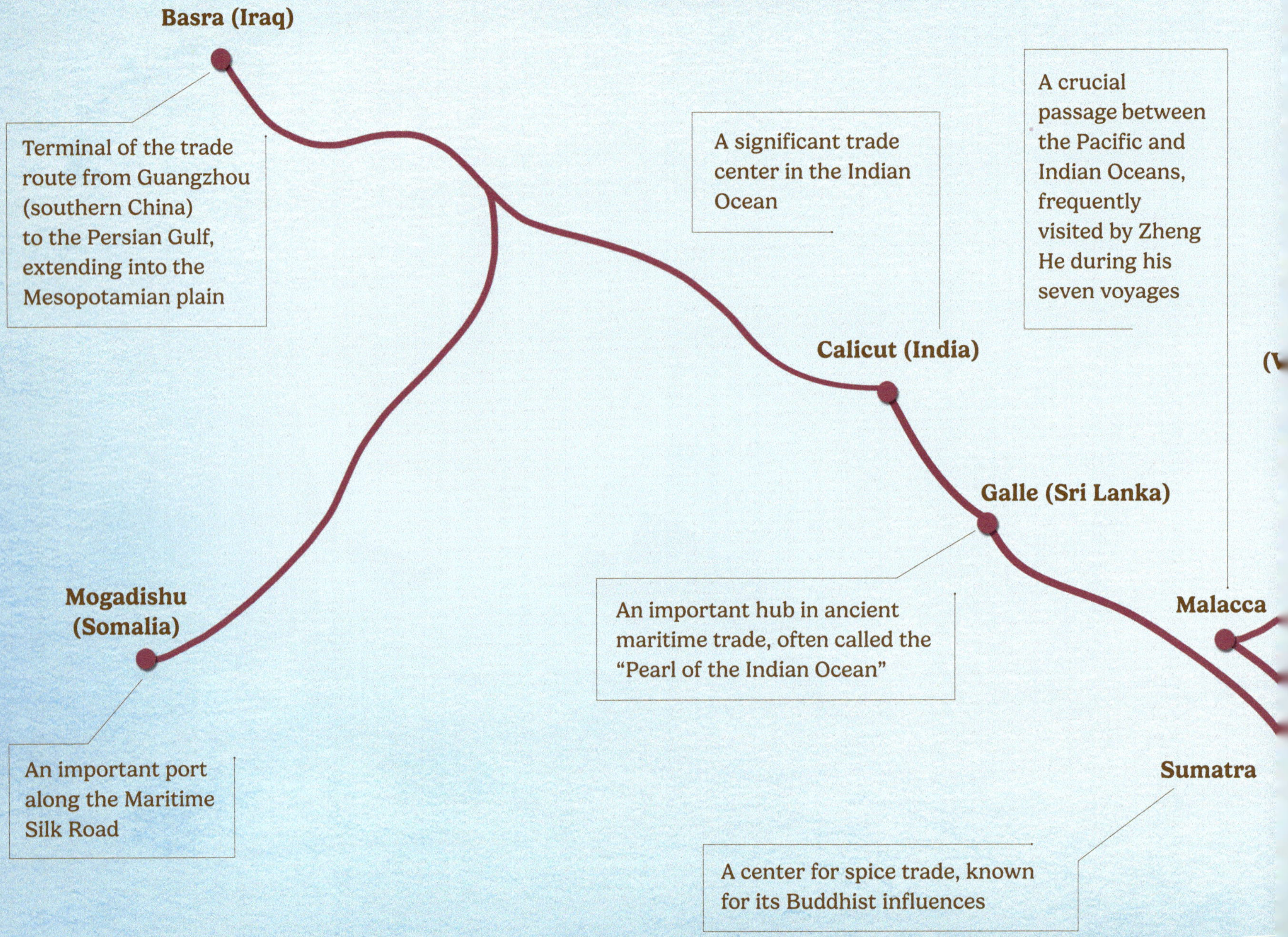

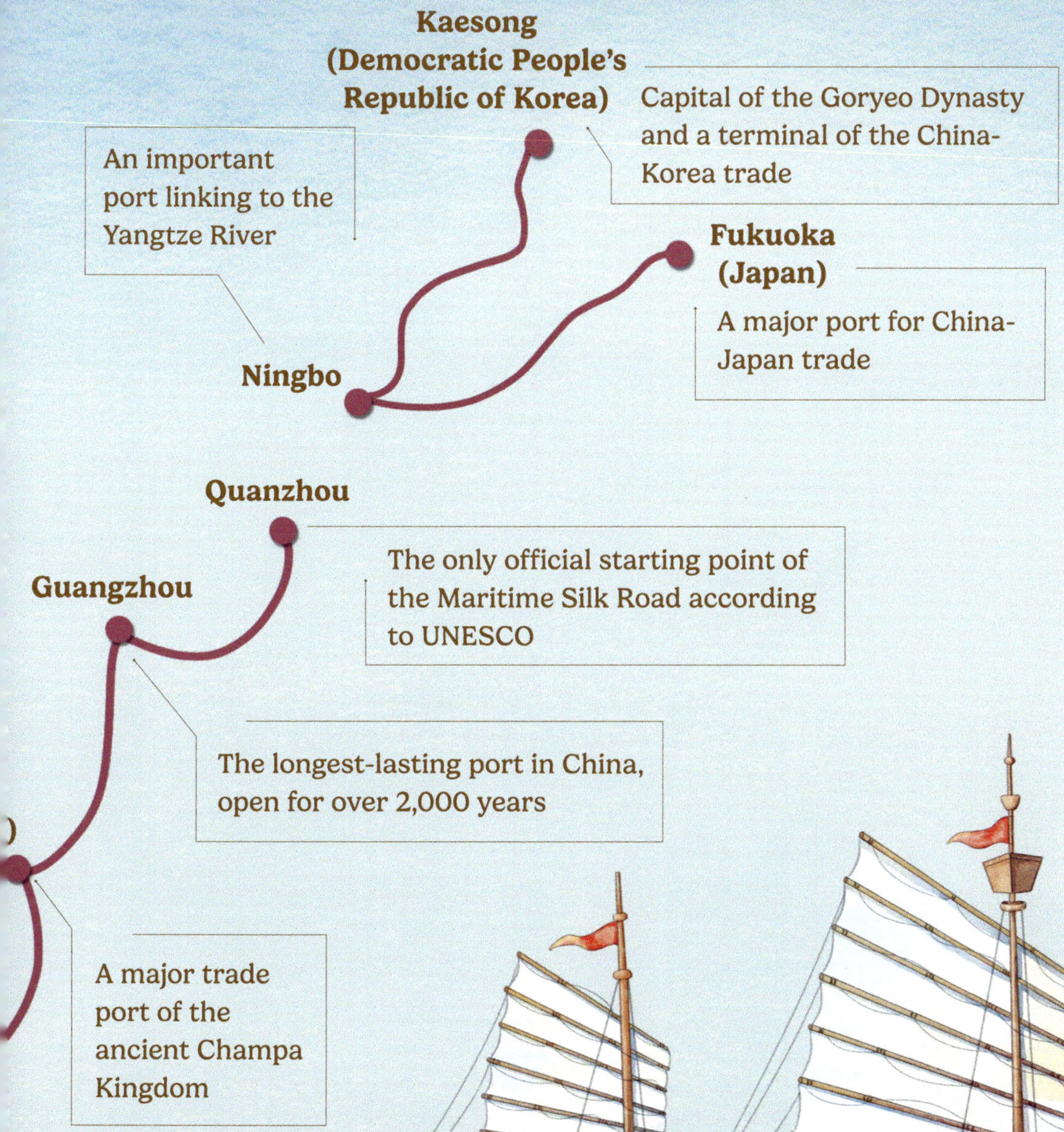

During the Song Dynasty, most people and cities were concentrated in the southern part of China. Larger ships were constructed to facilitate longer voyages, allowing porcelain to be transported in vast quantities to regions such as South Asia and Africa. After the Renaissance and the Age of Discovery, the porcelain trade surged, and it began entering Europe. This exchange also carried Chinese culture and innovations to the West.

Once porcelain was introduced to Europe, it gained immediate fame and high praise. The King of Spain even used Chinese porcelain to decorate his palace as a symbol of status and wealth.

The Polish King Augustus II was particularly enamored with Chinese porcelain. He is said to have exchanged 600 brave Saxon warriors with the King of Prussia to obtain more of it.

The emperors of the Yuan Dynasty (AD 1271–1368) had a particular fondness for white and blue porcelain. As a result, a type of porcelain with a white base and blue designs became widely popular. This style became known as blue-and-white porcelain.

In Western Asia, blue-and-white porcelain was considered a luxury, used only on special occasions. At grand banquets, nobles would serve food in blue-and-white porcelain bowls, symbolizing their wealth and status.

Europeans, eager to acquire porcelain, often commissioned custom pieces, with Chinese craftsmen creating porcelain items based on foreign merchants' requests and even incorporating advertisements into the designs.

In the 15th century, driven by the pursuit of gold, silver, and porcelain, Europeans embarked on the Age of Discovery and began expanding their colonial empires. As their wealth grew, they also witnessed the onset of the Industrial Revolution.

In the late 17th and early 18th centuries, European ships began making direct voyages to Guangzhou. A large amount of Chinese porcelain flooded the European market and became an integral part of daily life in European homes.

Europeans developed a deep admiration for porcelain and integrated it into many aspects of culture, including art, architecture, and fashion.

Porcelain became a staple of courtly decoration in Europe. Inspired by Chinese porcelain paintings, French artists created the Rococo art style, which was characterized by intricate designs and fine-line decorations. The influence of porcelain on European architecture can still be seen today.

The trade in porcelain also introduced Western painting techniques and other new technologies to China. These foreign influences played a crucial role in the evolution of Chinese porcelain. During this period, new styles like enamel-painted porcelain emerged.

Later, the enamel techniques were applied to metal products, giving rise to enamelware. Affordable and visually striking, enamelware became common in households by the 1980s, with cups and bowls crafted from this material.

Initially, porcelain was produced only in China, and countries outside of China had to pay high prices for it. As a result, other nations began imitating Chinese porcelain, striving to produce it domestically. This led to the creation of unique types of porcelain.

In Europe, due to the lack of high-quality clay, bone ash was used, leading to the invention of bone china.

Japanese porcelain, heavily influenced by Chinese techniques, incorporated local art styles, resulting in unique varieties such as Arita ware and Mino ware.

As an inorganic material, porcelain plays a significant role in modern society.

Porcelain knives, as thin as paper yet extremely sharp, are used in various applications.

The insulation devices on high-voltage poles are often made from porcelain, ensuring durability and resistance to extreme conditions.

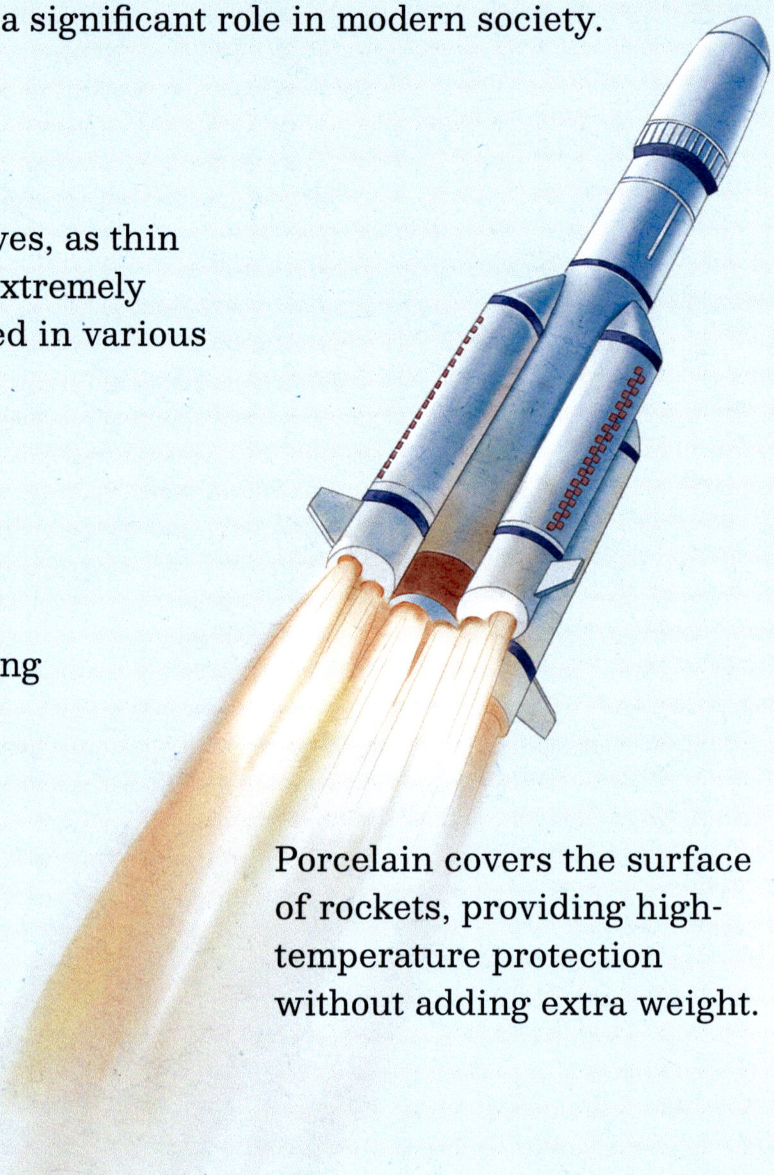

Porcelain covers the surface of rockets, providing high-temperature protection without adding extra weight.

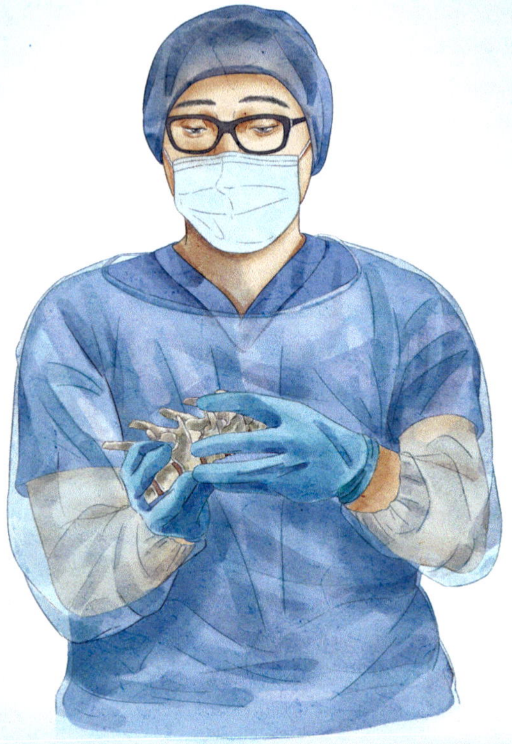

Scientists have discovered that porcelain possesses exceptional properties, including temperature resistance, high hardness, oxidation resistance, and excellent insulation. These attributes make it essential in high-tech fields, from small electronic components to large rocket engines.

Porcelain has also found a place in medicine. Scientists have combined it with nanotechnology to create nano-ceramics, which hold promise for treating certain diseases.

Porcelain is a remarkable representative of Chinese culture. Since its inception, it has continuously contributed to the world, and its combination with modern technology allows this ancient craft to shine in the contemporary era, benefiting people worldwide.

Annex: Colorful Porcelain

Cowpea-red glaze *zun* with floral and *chi*-dragon patterns (red)

Watermelon-green glaze straight-neck bottle (green)

Sweet white bowl with lotus patterns (white)

Rice-yellow glaze bowl with white cloud and dragon patterns (yellow)

Plum-green glaze spittoon from the Longquan Kiln (light green)

Peacock-green glaze *zun* with incised banana leaf and *taotie* patterns (blue)

Black glaze brush pot with gilded landscape and figure patterns (black)

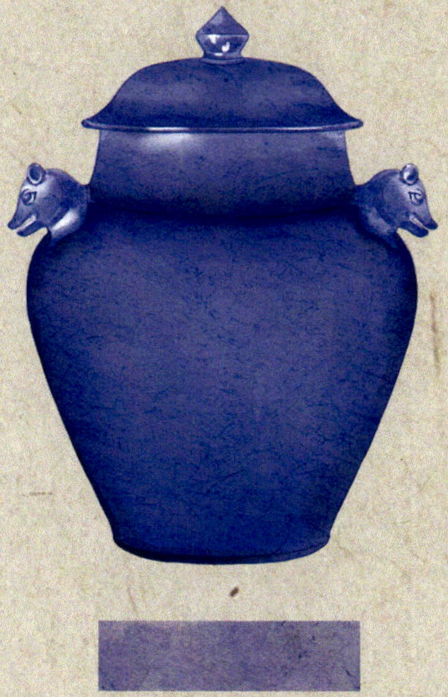

Eggplant-purple glaze lidded jar with animal ears (purple)

Chinese Stories: Four Major Contributions

Chinese Porcelain

Edited by Li Chaodong
Illustrated by Xu Meng
Translated by Mingjiu Qi and Yan Wu

First published in 2024 by Royal Collins Publishing Group Inc.
Groupe Publication Royal Collins Inc.
550-555 boul. René-Lévesque O Montréal (Québec) H2Z1B1 Canada

10 9 8 7 6 5 4 3 2 1

ISBN: 978-1-4878-1327-7

To find out more about our publications, please visit www.royalcollins.com.

About the Editor

LI CHAODONG, born in 1963, is a prominent figure in China's education publishing industry and a graduate of the Department of History at East China Normal University. Over his distinguished career, he has edited and published more than 50 book series. He has been honored as a "National Leading Talent in Press and Publication" and recognized as "China's Annual Publication Figure." Li currently serves as the Founding Vice President of the All-China Federation of Industry and Commerce Book Industry Chamber of Commerce, Vice President of the Fifth Council of the China Book Publishing Association, and Vice Chairman of both the Anhui and Jiangsu Publishing Associations.